THE SECOND BOOK OF CATHOLIC JOKES

Deacon Tom Sheridan

Foreword by Father Paul Boudreau

acta
PUBLICATIONS

THE BOOK OF CATHOLIC JOKES
by Deacon Tom Sheridan
with a Foreword by Father Paul Boudreau

Edited by Gregory F. Augustine Pierce
Editorial assistance by Mary Eggert, Donna Ryding, and Mary Pierce
Cover design by Tom A. Wright
Text design and typesetting by Patricia A. Lynch

Published by ACTA Publications, 4848 N. Clark Street, Chicago, IL 60640, (800) 397-2282, www.actapublications.com

Library of Congress Catalog number: 2010927567
ISBN: 978-0-87946-425-7
Printed in the United States of America by Total Printing Systems
Year 20 19 18 17 16 15 14 13
Printing 10 9 8 7 6 5 4 3 2

♻ Text printed on 30% post-consumer recycled paper

CONTENTS

DEDICATION

This book is dedicated to Kathy Sheridan,
who has made me smile for 45 years
but who still doesn't always appreciate my humor.

FOREWORD
by Father Paul Boudreau

There's nothing like a good joke to start off a sermon. When the preacher puts down the book and looks out at the congregation, the first thing he says is mighty important. If it starts off with "A priest, a minister, and a rabbi walk into a bar..." all the better. Hey, even if the rest of the homily is a stinker, at least you come away with your funny bone tickled.

I've been a preacher for almost 30 years. I know from experience that people don't remember what I tell them about the salvation of their immortal souls. But they remember the gags. Ten years down the road they'll remind me not of my profound utterances but of something I said that they thought was funny and never forgot.

Often the preacher himself is the favorite butt of a joke. That's the frosting on the cake for Catholics. God, you see, designed Catholic clergy for yucks. If the joke has a Henny Youngman-esque punch line like, "That was no lady; that was my bishop!" or the one where the drunk says to the deacon swinging the censor, "I love your dress but your purse is on fire," the laugh track in church goes way up.

Catholicism lends itself so well to humor. I mean, what a source of material: mystical encounters, miracles, unusual rituals, funny hats, unique hardware, all kinds of devotional tchotchkes, wife-less leaders, saints that fly and find your keys, angels, funerals, confessions, and — my favorite — the women religious.

Ah, the good sisters. Oh do we love to tease them. They are the pious women of our youth who have done so much to make the world a better place. But when we connect them to drinking, smoking, cussing, running around after dark, and other nefarious activities, what a riot.

You don't even have to tell a joke to be funny in a Catholic church. Like the lector at Mass who reads from "Saint Paul's letter to the Filipinos," or the infamous "flaming brassiere" passage from Genesis 15:17.

Deacon Tom Sheridan has a million of 'em. His first book, *The Book of Catholic Jokes*, published by ACTA, was brilliant. My favorite from that edition was a quick riddle that catches the humor in our Catholic perception of other religions: What do you get when you cross a Unitarian with a Jehovah's Witness? Someone who goes around ringing doorbells for no apparent reason.

I especially liked the golf jokes, of which there were plenty. That's because I minister in a land of golf courses and golf people. They love it when Jesus and Moses play a round and Jesus hits into the water. With this twosome—that can both divide the water and walk on it—there's always a punch line lurking just off the next tee. For example, Moses says: "He IS Jesus Christ. He THINKS he's Arnold Palmer."

And take our Bible…please. (Thank you, Henny.) What other religious text has the story of Balaam's ass, the talking donkey in Numbers 22? Or the bride in the Book of Tobit whose seven attempts at marriage all end with the mysterious death of the groom in the bridal chamber on the wedding night? Or the grumpy prophet in 2 Kings who sics hungry bears on a group of unruly children? Or the numerous gospel stories about the fishermen who can't catch fish? And, when they do, it's a miracle!

Catholic confession is a great context for jokes. I know. I'm the guy on the other side of the curtain. Deacon Tom cracked me up in this book with the one about the guy who confesses stealing so much lumber that the priest makes him promise to make a novena in penance. "I don't know what a novena is," the guy says, "but if you've got the blueprints, I've got the lumber."

Some of these you've undoubtedly heard before. I've heard most of them. People can't resist telling the parish priest the latest Catholic joke. That's how Deacon Tom gets most of his material. We clergy are like the cloistered monks who repeat the same jokes to each other so often over the years that they now just number each of them. "Number 323," one will shout in the middle of the silent meal, and everyone breaks up. We priests have heard the same jokes so many times that now a whole long story can be summed up in a one-sentence punch line: "Then I just confirmed the bats and they never came back to the church!"

Maybe you haven't heard that one. Or maybe you haven't yet met Little Jonnie, the Catholic eight-year-old who is the star of many of these jokes. If not, then I suggest you dig right in to *The Second Book of Catholic Jokes* (where DOES Deacon Tom get those snappy titles?). This book has more funny jokes in it than a barrel of Irish cops, and you can quote me on that.

INTRODUCTION

Someone's bound to ask: How dare I make jokes about the church?

Okay, here's why: Our human attempts to understand God and God's action in the world are hilarious. When we forget that very powerful truth, we risk losing our real connection to the divine.

The life God gives us can be very humorous. Comical. Downright laughable. Despite that, there are lots of very religious people running around these days with frowns on their faces, with grimness in their hearts, and words like "don't you dare…" on their lips.

How sad. But don't take my word for it. No less than the inestimable Archbishop Fulton J. Sheen, that celebrated evangelist of airwaves, said in a 1959 broadcast that Jesus had a "divine sense of humor." Sheen said, "There was nothing in this world that he ever took seriously — except the salvation of souls."

Not convinced? Still think that religion means having a dour outlook on life? Count the priests, deacons, and occasional male or female religious or layperson you know who use jokes and other humor in their homilies because they present an outlook on life we can all relate to. After all, we humans can be the funniest of all God's creatures, without even trying.

Archbishop Sheen used humor to reach into the hearts, minds, and souls of the millions who were touched by his broadcasts. More than 30 years after Sheen's death, his stories — some of them really no more than long jokes — still resonate. Here's one. He said that at one parish where he was preaching there would be an envelope in the collection with a note: "IOU $35" or "IOU $50." This went on for weeks. Finally there was an envelope filled with cash, the total of all the IOUs. Sheen said he felt good about his preaching until the following week, when there was another envelope. This time, the note read: "You owe me $25."

Still not convinced?

Even the Vatican's newspaper, *L'Osservatore Romano*, says that it appreciates the jokes and humor in "The Simpsons," as irreverent and comical a slice of exaggerated life as ever existed. When the animated TV show marked its 20th anniversary in 2009, the pope's semi-official publication commented that without Homer Simpson and his often befuddled and sarcastic pals "many today wouldn't know how to laugh."

If that's not a character reference for religious humor, I don't know what is.

Humor is very malleable. In researching thousands of jokes, some suitable for publication in this book and others not, one thing became clear to me: There's a thread of humor running through nearly all faiths. In fact, many of the jokes in this book began in one faith tradition and "swam the Tiber" to find a home among Catholics. Undoubtedly, many have swum the other direction as well. (For example, a Mormon newspaper writer in Salt Lake City took several of the jokes from my first book of Catholic jokes, changed all the characters to Mormons, and published them in his review of my book. They all worked just fine.)

While the majority of jokes in this volume have a Catholic slant, others look at our sometimes warped understandings of God, the Bible, the afterlife, and even other faiths and denominations. Always with a smile, of course, and all done in the spirit of love.

In other words, "Godly" humor is ecumenical and interfaith.

The question for religious people is always whether or not we have the courage — and the faith — to laugh at our own foibles and pretensions and not, as Archbishop Sheen warned us against, take ourselves so seriously all the time.

ABOUT THESE JOKES

Religion offers a great treasury of humor. This is the second volume of Catholic jokes. Like the first book, the jokes gathered here have been collected from friends and other contributors, gleaned — and often polished — from various websites and other sources. Versions may be new or been circulated for ages. Some have been adapted from ones perhaps not specifically dealing with religion, but surely focused on the human condition that Catholics, despite some evidence to the contrary, share with everyone else.

As stated in the first *Book of Catholic Jokes*, I believe all these jokes to be in what the lawyers call the "public domain," but if authorship or copyright of a particular joke can be determined, please let the editors know so it can be corrected and they can go to jail.

Will there be a third volume of Catholic jokes? Haven't you heard the one about the Trinity? So if you've got a favorite joke that you'd like to submit for the next edition, please mail it to:

Deacon Tom Sheridan
The Book of Catholic Jokes
c/o ACTA Publications
4848 N. Clark Street
Chicago, IL 60640
800-397-2282
acta@actapublications.com
www.actapublications.com

THE JOKES

For Catholics, celibacy can be a choice in life, or it can be a condition imposed by circumstances.

While attending a Marriage Preparation Weekend, Walter and his future wife, Ann, listened to the instructor declare, "It is essential that husbands and wives know the little things that are important to each other."

The instructor then addressed the men: "Guys, can you name your wife's favorite flower?"

Walter leaned over, touched Ann's arm gently, and whispered, "Gold Medal All Purpose, isn't it?"

Thus began Walter's life of celibacy.

Little Jonnie had been exceedingly naughty, and during dinner he was forced to eat alone in the corner at a card table. When everyone was seated, his father bowed his head and gave thanks.

Then little Jonnie gravely bowed his head and prayed out loud, "Thank you, Lord, for preparing a table for me in the presence of my enemies."

Why do they say "amen" at the end of a prayer instead of "awomen?"

The same reason they sing hymns instead of hers.

A Catholic couple in Chicago made plans to visit Florida in order to thaw out during a particularly cold winter in the Windy City. They planned to stay at the same hotel where they had honeymooned two decades before.

Their busy schedules, however, made it impossible for the couple to travel together. So the husband flew to Florida on Thursday, and his wife planned to arrive the following day. The husband checked into the hotel and decided to email his wife from the hotel's business center. However, he mistyped her email address.

Meanwhile in Dallas, a widow who had just returned home from her husband's funeral checked her email, expecting messages of condolences from relatives and friends. She read the first message, screamed, and fainted.

The widow's son rushed into the room, found his mother on the floor, and saw this on the computer screen:

To: My Loving Wife
From: Your Departed Husband
Subject: I've arrived

I know you're surprised to hear from me so soon, but they have computers here now and I thought I'd let you know I'm already here and have been checked in.

Everything is ready for your arrival tomorrow.

PS: Sure is hot down here!

Over coffee and donuts after Mass one Sunday, an engineer, a physician, and a politician were arguing over whose profession was the oldest. Not surprisingly, they ended up discussing God, creation, and the Garden of Eden.

The doctor boasted that medicine was the oldest profession, citing the creation of Eve in the Garden of Eden. "Taking a rib from Adam's side was a major surgery," he said. "There's no profession older than mine."

The engineer didn't give up easily. "Before Adam and Eve were created," he said, "the chaos had to be organized and set in good order. That's an engineer's job. My profession is even older than the Garden of Eden."

The politician just smirked and asked, "Guess who created the chaos?"

One Sunday morning, a mother was sending her eight-year-old son, little Jonnie, off to Mass by himself. She gave the boy two dollars.

"One is to put in the collection plate and the other is for you to buy a candy bar for yourself on your way home," she said.

Little Jonnie went on his way walking to church, with a dollar in each hand, when all of sudden he dropped one and it fell right down into a sewer drain. Little Jonnie looked down but couldn't see where it had gone. He got up, brushed off his pant knees, and said, "Sorry, Lord, I just lost your dollar."

As the old monk lay dying, the abbot asked him, "Dear Brother, do you have any wish before you die?"

"Well, Father Abbot," said the dying man softly, "I've lived all my life here in the monastery and have seen nothing of the world. There are two things I'd like to touch before I die."

"Of course," replied the abbot, "what are they?

With a quavering voice, the monk asked, "I've just heard about these but I've never seen either of them. One is a woman and the other is a bicycle."

Getting a bicycle was not difficult, but the abbot wasn't sure how to fulfill the dying monk's other request. So the abbot brought a brand new bike into the infirmary and set it up in the middle of the room: "Here it is, Brother. What do you think?"

The dying old man squealed with great delight, looking over and touching each and every shiny part of the bike for long time.

When he finished, the old man said, "Thank you, Father Abbot. I think you can skip the bicycle."

———

**Catholics are funny;
we all want to be in the front of the bus,
the middle of the road,
and the back of the church.**

It had been a while since Joe had sought the Sacrament of Reconciliation. But one day he wandered into an unfamiliar church and entered the confessional. He was surprised how much things had changed. On one wall there was a fully equipped bar with Guinness on tap. On the other wall there was a dazzling array of the finest Cuban cigars.

When the pastor came in, Joe began the old ritual: "Father, forgive me, it's been a very long time since I've been to confession, but I must first say that the confessional is much more inviting these days."

The priest replied: "You're on my side."

A Jesuit, a Dominican, and a Trappist were marooned on a desert island. Under a palm tree they discovered a magic lamp.

Skeptical, they rubbed it and, sure enough, a genie appeared and offered them three wishes. Since there were three of them, they decided that it would be fair for each to get one wish.

The Jesuit thought for a moment and said he wanted to teach at the world's most famous university. Poof, he was gone!

The Dominican wished to preach in the world's largest church. Poof, he was gone too!

The Trappist looked around and thought, "Gee, I already got my wish."

Like many young men, the deacon's teenage son didn't really know what he wanted to do when he grew up. While the son didn't seem too concerned about it, his father was. One day, his father decided to try an experiment. He placed four objects on his son's desk: a Bible, a $10 bill, a bottle of whiskey, and a *Playboy* magazine.

"When my son comes home from school, I'll see which he picks up," the deacon said to himself. "If it's the Bible, he's going to be a priest or a deacon. What a blessing that would be! If he picks up the money, he's going into business. That'd be Okay, too. But if he picks up the bottle, he's going to be a no-good drunken bum. Lord, what a shame that would be. Worst of all, if he picks up that magazine he's going to be a skirt-chasing womanizer. I don't think I could tolerate that."

When the boy came home, he tossed his books on the bed and spotted the four objects. He put the Bible under his arm, slipped the $10 into his pocket, uncorked the bottle and took a big swig, and started paging through the magazine.

"Lord have mercy," whispered the deacon to himself, "he's gonna run for Congress."

Why did God create man before woman?

Because God didn't want to have to listen to any advice.

While picking up groceries for their convent on a scorching hot afternoon, two sisters in full habit happened to pass by the liquor section.

One asked the other if she would like some beer that evening. The second nun agreed that, indeed, it would be very nice to have a glass or two of beer on such a hot night, but she conceded that she would feel uncomfortable about buying it.

"No problem," said the first sister. She picked up a six-pack and took it to the cashier, a young man who looked more than a little surprised.

"This is for washing our hair," the sister told him.

Without blinking an eye, the cashier threw a bag of pretzels in the bag with the beer.

"The curlers are on me, S'ter," he said with a smile.

Three fundamental truths about recognition:

1. Jews and Muslims don't recognize Jesus as the Son of God.

2. Protestants don't recognize the pope as the Vicar of Christ.

3. Baptists don't recognize each other at the bar on Saturday nights.

It was a packed church at Bill and Maryanne's wedding Mass. The priest who was going to say the Mass decided that since he had a few minutes to spare he would take a walk out to the entrance of the church where the bride was waiting.

"Well, Maryanne, how you doing on your special day?" he asked the bride.

"Okay, I guess, Father," she replied. "I'm just nervous to have to walk down that long aisle with my dad."

"I'll share a little secret with you," the priest said, "one that I've heard brides use over the years. As you start to walk down the aisle, look straight ahead and think how wonderful the white runner looks. Then look to the altar and see all the beautiful flowers. Finally, listen to the hymn being played as you march down the aisle. You'll be up there before you know it."

Then the priest went back to the sacristy, the organ started the wedding march, the bride breathed a deep sigh and started down the aisle, saying to herself just loud enough so her father could hear her: "Aisle...altar...hymn. Aisle...altar...hymn. Aisle...altar...hymn."

Why did Moses wander the desert for 40 years?

He left his Promised Land GPS back in Egypt.

One morning a lame man struggled into a Catholic church. He stopped in front of the holy water font, splashed some on both legs, and then threw away his crutches.

An altar boy witnessed the scene and rushed into the rectory to tell the pastor what he'd just seen.

"Son, you've just witnessed a miracle!" the priest cried. "Tell me, where is this man now?"

"Flat on his back over by the holy water," the boy said.

Two cannibals are discussing recipes. The first says, "You know, I just can't seem to get a missionary tender. I've baked 'em; I've roasted 'em; I've stewed 'em; I've barbecued 'em. I've tried every sort of marinade on them. Nothing works."

The second cannibal asks, "What kind of missionary do you use?"

The other replies, "You know, the ones that have those brown cloaks with a rope around the waist and they're sort of bald on top."

"Ah!" the second cannibal replies. "That's your problem. Those are friars!"

Doctor: "Your recovery was a miracle!"

Patient: "Thank God! Does that mean I don't have to pay your bill?"

Little Jonnie was in church one Sunday with his mother, when he began to feel ill. "Mommy," he asked, "can we leave now?"

"No," his mother replied. "Why?"

"I think I have to throw up!"

"Then go out the front door and around to the back of the church and throw up behind a bush," she said.

Little Jonnie left, but he returned just a few seconds later.

"Did you throw up?" Mom asked.

"Yes," said little Jonnie.

"How could you get back so quickly?"

"I didn't have to go out of the church, Mommy. They have a box next to the front door that says, 'For the Sick.'"

A pious man who had reached the age of 105 suddenly stopped going to Mass.

Alarmed by the fellow's absence after so many years of faithful attendance, the pastor went to see him. He found him in excellent health, so the priest asked, "How come after all these years we don't see you at Mass anymore?"

The old man lowered his voice. "I'll tell you, Father," he whispered. "When I got to be 90, I expected God to take me any day. But then I got to be 95, then 100, then 105. So, I figured that God is very busy and must've forgotten about me, and I don't want to remind him."

An avid golfer finally gets his once-in-a-lifetime chance for an audience with the pope. After standing in line for hours, he meets the pope and asks, "Holiness, I have a question that only you can answer. You see, I love golf, and I feel a real need to know if there is a golf course in heaven. Can you tell me if there is?"

The pope considers for a moment, and says, "I do not know the answer to your question, my son, but I will talk to God and get back to you."

The following day the man is summoned for a private audience with the pope. "My son, I have some good news and some bad news in relation to your question. The good news is that heaven has the most fabulous golf course that you could imagine and is in eternally perfect shape."

"And what's the bad news?" asks the man.

"You tee off tomorrow morning at 8:00."

———

The pastor of an old German parish in Milwaukee wasn't about to let the recent economic downturn destroy tradition. Even though the town was hurting from the recession, the parish's annual WienerFest had always been a big morale booster for the whole community. Despite grumbling from the parish council, the pastor repackaged the festival. The new theme: "It was the best of times; it was the wurst of times."

A Lutheran pastor is walking around his neighborhood when he sees several children playing with some newborn puppies.

"Kids, what kind of puppies are these?" he asks.

"Well they're Lutheran puppies, of course," reply the kids.

The pastor is really touched. A few days later he sees the children and again asks what kind of puppies they have. And again he's assured they are Lutheran puppies.

About a week later, the pastor's bishop comes for a visit. Hoping to impress her, the pastor takes her for a walk by the children with the puppies. He proudly asks them, "Children, what type of puppies are these?"

"Why, they are Catholic puppies, of course!" they reply.

The pastor turns beet red, demanding, "But last week and the time before that you told me they were Lutheran puppies!"

"Yes, but their eyes are open now," reply the kids.

———

A murderer is about to be executed in the electric chair.

"Have you any last requests?" asked the chaplain.

"Yes, Father," replies the murderer. "Will you hold my hand?"

A priest went up to a logging area in the Great Northwest to hear confessions. When he arrived there was a long line of tough-looking guys, so he sat down in the confessional and waited for the first one.

The first logger knelt down and said gruffly, "Well, Father, I've been really bad. I've broken just about every commandment in the book."

The priest asked him, "Well, have you committed murder?"

The lumberjack conceded that he hadn't committed murder. Considering the large number of confessions still to go, the priest told the logger just to say an "Our Father" and try to avoid sin in the future.

The confused logger came out and hollered to his buddies, "Forget it, guys. He's only interested in hearing murder cases today."

Fifteen men remained in line.

———

A New York-bound jetliner was bouncing through heavy weather. As the passengers were being jostled by the turbulence a young woman turned to the priest sitting next to her and with a nervous laugh asked him, "Father, you're a man of God. Can't you do something about this storm?"

The priest looked at her and replied, "Lady, I'm in sales, not management."

An Augustinian, a Franciscan, and a Jesuit die and end up at the Pearly Gates together. Jesus asks each, "If you could go back, what would you change?"

The Augustinian ponders for a minute and says, "There's so much sin in the world. If I went back, I'd try and make people behave better."

The Franciscan also thinks a bit and says, "There's so much poverty in the world. If I went back, I'd try and get people to share more of their wealth with the poor."

The Jesuit looks at Jesus and quickly replies, "If I went back, I'd change doctors."

A pastor was worried about how he was going to ask the parish to come up with the money to cover unexpected repairs to the roof of the church. Before Mass, the new organist asked him what music she was to play.

"Here's a copy of the hymn list," he said impatiently. "But you'll have to think of something to play after I make the announcement about the finances."

After the homily, the priest paused and then announced, "I am sorry to say this, but we are in great difficulty. The roof repairs cost twice as much as we expected, and we need $4,000 more. Any of you who can pledge another $100 or more, please stand."

At that moment, the organist started playing "The Star Spangled Banner."

Mass was going smoothly when suddenly a flash of light and smoke appeared in front of the pulpit followed by a large "BOOM!"

When the smoke cleared, the astonished congregation saw a familiar red figure on the altar, complete with horns, pitchfork, and tail.

Immediately, panic set in. People crowded through the doors, trampling each other in their rush to get away.

Satan watched with great glee, but then he spotted one parishioner still lounging comfortably in his pew.

"Do you not know who I am?" thundered Satan.

"Sure I do," the man replied calmly.

Satan was puzzled. "Do you not fear me?"

"Nope."

"Why not?"

The man snorted, "Why should I? I've been married to your sister for 35 years!"

When was the longest day in the Bible?

The day Adam was created.

Why?

Because there was no Eve.

There were once two evil brothers. They were rich and used their money to hide their dastardly ways from the public eye. They even attended the same parish and looked to be perfect Catholics.

Their pastor, however, was not fooled.

One of the brothers died. The other brother called on the pastor the day before the funeral and handed him a huge check, enough to pay off the new addition to the church that was being built.

"I have only one condition," he said. "At his funeral, you must say my brother was a saint."

The pastor thought for a moment and agreed.

At the funeral, the pastor was unrestrained: "This was an evil man. He cheated on his wife and abused his family." At the end, however, the priest concluded, "But compared to his brother, he was a saint."

A young Catholic woman brings her fiancé to meet her parents. The father invites the young man into his study for a talk.

"So, what are your plans?" the father asks.

"I'm a scripture scholar," the groom-to-be replies.

"A scripture scholar? Hmmm," the father says. "Admirable, but how will you provide for my daughter?"

"I will study," the young man replies, "and God will provide for us."

"And how will you buy her a home such as she deserves?" asks the father.

"I will concentrate on my studies," the young man replies, "and God will provide for us."

"And children?" asks the father. "How will you support children?"

"Don't worry, sir, God will provide," replies the man.

Later, the girl's mother asks her husband, "How did your talk go?"

The father answers, "He has no job, no plans, and no prospects. But the good news is that he thinks I'm God."

––––––––

A rabbi, an imam, and a priest are playing poker when police raid the game.

Turning to the Muslim, the cop asks: "Imam, were you gambling?" Turning his eyes to heaven, the imam whispers, "Allah, forgive me for what I am about to do." To the officer he then says, "No, officer, I was not gambling."

The officer then asks the priest: "Father, were you gambling?" Again, after an appeal to God, the priest replies, "No, officer, I was not gambling."

Turning to the rabbi, the officer asks: "Rabbi, were you gambling?" Looking around and shrugging his shoulders, the rabbi replies, "So, with whom would I have been gambling?"

A woman had been in business for many years, but the business is going down the drain. She is seriously depressed and doesn't know what to do, so she goes to her pastor for advice.

The priest tells her, "Take a beach chair and a Bible and drive down to the edge of the ocean. Take the beach chair and sit on it, and take the Bible out and open it. The wind will riffle the pages for a while and eventually the Bible will stay open at a particular page. Read the first words your eyes fall on and they will tell you what to do."

The woman agrees. So she sits in a beach chair at the water's edge and opens her Bible. The wind riffles the pages and then stops. She looks down at the Bible and her eyes fall on words that tell her exactly what she has to do.

Three months later the woman comes back to see the priest. She is wearing a $1,000 Italian suit, has on a beautiful diamond necklace, and looks great. Not a trace of depression in her face. She hands the pastor a thick envelope of money and tells him it's for the parish because of the great advice he gave her.

The priest is delighted and asks what words in the Bible brought her such good fortune.

The woman replies: "The Good Book opened to 'Chapter 11.'"

———

**Opportunity may knock once,
but temptation bangs on the door forever.**

Two women religious are vacationing in Europe, passing through Transylvania. Despite warnings, they've stayed out after dark. Sure enough, as they're driving along, a vampire flies out of the night and lands on their windshield, hissing and baring his fangs.

"Dear Lord! What shall we do?" cries the first nun.

"Turn on the windshield wipers," yells the second nun. "Maybe that'll break his grip."

No luck, but now the vampire is wet and angry.

"What shall we do now?" yells the first nun, even more frightened.

"Weave the car back and forth. Maybe he'll fall off," says the second.

No luck. The vampire is beating on the glass now, and it's starting to crack.

"NOW WHAT?" cries the first nun.

The second nun has a sudden flash of insight. "Show him your cross!" she yells.

The first nun sticks her head out the window and yells, "Get off my car, you foul little vampire, before I smack you with my ruler!"

Why didn't Noah ever go fishing?

He only had two worms.

Every time a pope is elected, there are many ancient rituals and ceremonies in accordance with tradition.

There is one tradition few people know about, however. Shortly after the new pope is enthroned, the chief rabbi of Rome seeks an audience. He presents the pope with a silver tray bearing a velvet cushion. On top of the cushion is an ancient, shriveled parchment envelope. The pope symbolically stretches out his arm in a gesture of rejection. The chief rabbi leaves, taking the envelope with him, and does not return until the next pope is elected.

Pope Benedict XVI was intrigued by this ritual, the origins of which were unknown to him. He instructed Vatican scholars to research it, but they came up with nothing. When the time came and the chief rabbi arrived for his audience, the new pope faithfully enacted the ritual rejection, but as the chief rabbi turned to leave, the pope called him back.

"My brother," the holy father whispered, "I must confess that we are ignorant of the meaning of this ritual repeated for centuries with the representative of the Jewish people. I have to ask you, what's it all about?"

The chief rabbi shrugged and replied, "We have no more idea than you. The origin of the ceremony is lost in the mists of history."

The pope said, "Let us retire to my private chambers and enjoy a glass of wine together. Then, with your agreement, we shall open the envelope and discover the secret at last." The chief rabbi agreed. He was as curious as the pope.

When they were alone, the pope gingerly pried open the parchment envelope with trembling fingers, and the chief rabbi removed a folded sheet of ancient paper. It was written in ancient Aramaic.

"What does it say?" the pope asked.

"It's the bill for the Last Supper," said the rabbi.

———

A little girl walked to and from school daily. One day, though the weather that morning was okay, by afternoon the winds had whipped up, bringing thunder and lightning.

Soon, the thunder was roaring and the lightning flashed like a flaming sword, cutting through the sky. The little girl's mother was worried and got in her car and drove along the route to her child's school.

As she did, she saw her little girl walking along the sidewalk. At each flash of lightning, the child would stop, look up, and smile.

The mother pulled up next to her daughter, opened the door, and asked, "What are you doing, Honey? Why are you stopping and smiling every time there is lightning?"

The child answered, "God keeps taking pictures of me," the little girl said. "Don't you think he wants me to smile?"

———

Forbidden fruit creates many different kinds of jams.

A local Catholic pastor met three prominent Baptists on the golf course one day and invited them to come to his church as part of the town's ecumenical program. That Sunday, just as Mass was beginning, they all showed up.

The small church was already packed and there was no place for them to sit, but when the priest saw the three Baptists entering, he quickly leaned over to the deacon and whispered, "Please get three chairs for my Baptist friends."

The deacon, who was hard of hearing, leaned closer and said, "I beg your pardon?"

"Get three chairs for my Baptist friends," repeated the priest. The deacon strained closer with a puzzled look still on his face.

Once more the priest tried, speaking slowly and distinctly. "Get three chairs for the Baptists," he said.

The deacon's face lit up in comprehension, and he turned to the congregation. "All right, everybody," he called out, "three cheers for the Baptists!"

**Archbishop Fulton J. Sheen once said
that hearing most nuns' confessions
was like being pelted to death with popcorn.**

For years before she died, the woman had been a thorn in the side of just about everyone in the parish, including the pastor and parish staff. Not to mention her husband. At her funeral, just as the deacon was concluding the burial service, a violent storm broke out. The final blessing was drowned out by a huge clap of thunder, and lightning cut the power in the church for a second. The woman's long-suffering husband looked up from his pew and said to no one in particular: "Well, at least we know that Mildred's arrived."

——

A small plane full of retirees heading for Florida was gripped with fear when the pilot announced, "Two of our engines are on fire; we're flying through a heavy fog and it has eliminated virtually all our visibility."

The passengers were numb with fear, except for one…a retired deacon. "Now, folks, keep calm," he said. "Let's bow our heads and pray."

Immediately, the passengers bowed their heads to pray, all but one fellow near the front.

"Why aren't you praying?" asked the deacon.

"I don't know how to pray," replied the passenger.

"Well, just do something religious!" piped up another passenger.

So the man got up and started walking up and down the aisle, taking up a collection.

One summer, a drought threatened the crop in a small town. On a hot and dry Sunday, the pastor told his Catholic congregation, "There isn't anything that will save us except to pray for rain. Go home, pray, believe, and come back next Sunday ready to thank God for sending rain."

The people did as they were told and returned to church the following Sunday. But as soon as the priest saw them, he was furious.

"We can't worship today. You do not yet believe," he said.

"But," they protested, "we prayed, and we do believe."

"Then where are your umbrellas?"

———

You might be a traditional Catholic if:

- You're sure the divine presence is strongest in the back three pews of church.

- You think someone who shouts "Amen" during the homily might be in the wrong church.

- You clapped after Mass when the liberal young priest said he was leaving the parish, and then felt guilty all week—not that you were glad he was going but because you had never clapped in church before and kind of liked it.

Several priests of various orders were celebrating a liturgy during a retreat. There were Franciscans, Benedictines, Dominicans, Carmelites, and Jesuits. Suddenly the lights of the retreat house dimmed and went out.

The Franciscans burst into a song praising God for the darkness.

The Benedictines continued the prayers from memory, without missing a beat.

The Dominicans began to discuss light as a signification of the transmission of divine knowledge.

The Carmelites fell into silence and started to practice slow, steady breathing.

The Jesuits sent one of their guys into the basement to replace the fuse.

A religious ed teacher challenged her children to take some time on Sunday afternoon following Mass to write a letter to God. They were to bring their letter back the following week.

One little boy wrote, "Dear God, We had a good time at church today. Wish you could have been there."

On the first day, God created the dog and then told it, "Sit all day by the door and bark at anyone who comes in or walks past. For this, I will give you a life span of 20 years."

The dog said, "That's a long time just to be barking. How about I live only 10 years and give you back the other 10?"

God said, "So be it."

On the second day, God created the monkey and said to it, "Entertain people, do tricks, and make them laugh. For this, I'll give you a 20-year life span."

The monkey said, "Do monkey tricks for 20 years? That's a pretty long time to be on stage. How about I live only 10 and give you back the other 10 like the dog did?"

And God said, "So be it."

On the third day, God created the cow and said to it, "You must go into the field with the farmer all day long and suffer under the sun, have calves and give milk to support the farmer's family. For this, I will give you a life span of 60 years."

The cow said, "That's a tough life you want to give me for 60 years. How about I live 20 and give you back the other 40?"

And again God said, "So be it."

On the fourth day, God created humans and said, "Eat, sleep, play, marry and enjoy your life. For this, I'll give you 20 years."

But the humans said, "Only 20 years? Life looks pretty good to us. Could you possibly give us our own 20, the cow's extra 40, the monkey's extra 10, and the dog's extra 10 as well? That would make 80 years. Okay?"

"Okay," said God. "So be it."

So now you know why, for our first 20 years, we eat, sleep, play, and enjoy ourselves. For the next 40 we slave in the sun. For the next 10 years, we do tricks to entertain our grandchildren. And for the last 10, we sit on the front porch and bark at everyone.

———

As part of an interfaith exchange program, a rabbi is invited to an evening meal at a Catholic monastery.

After a delightful meal one of the monks stands up and says, "281!"

There are a few quiet giggles, then another stands up and says, "356." Again more giggles.

Intrigued, the rabbi asks the abbot what the numbers mean.

"Well," says the abbot, "we've been living together for so long that we all know each other's jokes. So instead of repeating them, we've given them each a number. It's simply a way of saving time."

"Want to give it a try?" asks the abbot.

The rabbi stands up and shouts, "829!"

Whereupon all the monks collapse in fits of unrestrained laughter.

Finally, when the abbot is able to rein in his own exuberant giggling, the rabbi asks him, "Why was my joke so funny?"

"We hadn't heard that one before," says the abbot.

A man who had spent his life as a devout Christian dies. He's met at the gates of heaven by St. Peter, who begins to give him a tour of the wonderful place where he'll spend eternity.

As the tour goes on, St. Peter points out all the different Christian enclaves scattered around heaven. "There are the Baptists. Over here are the Lutherans. There are the Methodists, the Presbyterians, the Disciples of Christ…." Finally they approach one group way off by themselves. St. Peter motions for the man to come closer and whispers, "Now, as we pass by this next group, we need to be really unobtrusive. These are the Catholics, and they think they're the only ones here."

———

Why are some liberal Catholics such lousy singers?

They're always reading ahead to see if they agree with the next line.

———

Two guys on really high scaffolds are painting the ceiling of a church. They look down and see a little old lady kneeling in prayer right below them. One of the painters decides to have a little fun and in his deepest voice says, "This is Jesus talking." Nothing happens. So he says again, "Woman, this is Jesus speaking to you." Finally the lady, still looking straight ahead, says, "Be quiet! I'm talking to your mother!"

A newly ordained deacon was so nervous he could hardly talk during his first homily. After Mass, he asked the pastor how he had done. The pastor replied, "When I'm worried about getting nervous in the pulpit, I put a little vodka in a glass instead of water. If I start to get nervous, I take a sip."

The following Sunday, the deacon took his pastor's advice. He was nervous so before beginning, he took several swallows. This time, his homily went smoothly, or so he thought. After Mass the deacon found the following note in the sacristy: You sip the vodka, not gulp it. And by the way, Jacob "wagered" his donkey; he did not "bet his ass."

———

A Lutheran pastor and his wife were driving along Chicago's Lake Shore Drive when flashing blue lights appeared in their rear-view mirror and they were pulled over for speeding. As Officer O'Malley approached the driver's side of the car, he spotted the pastor's collar, and mistook him for a Catholic priest.

"Oh, sorry about dat, fader. Uh, just try and slow it down a little, Okay?"

As they drove away, the pastor's wife said, "Shame on you, Harold! That was unethical. You know who he thought you were!" "Oh, I know who he thought *I* was," replied the pastor. "I'm just wondering who he thought *you* were."

A priest, a Pentecostal preacher, and a rabbi all served as chaplains to the students of a large public university in the Deep South.

They would get together two or three times a week for coffee and to talk shop. During their conversations, one of the clergymen commented that preaching to people isn't really all that hard. A real challenge would be to preach to a bear.

One thing led to another and the three decided to do an experiment. They would each go up separately to the Smoky Mountains, find a bear, and attempt to convert it.

The following week they gathered again to discuss their experiences.

Father Flannery, his arm in a sling, on crutches, and with various bandages on his body went first. "Well," he said, "I went into the woods to find a bear. And when I found him I began to read to him from the catechism. Well, that bear wanted nothing to do with me and began to slap me around. So, I quickly grabbed my holy water, sprinkled him with it, and he became as gentle as a lamb. The bishop is coming out next week to give him first communion and confirmation."

Rev. Billy Bob was up next. He was in a wheelchair, with an arm and both legs in casts, and an IV drip in his free arm. In his best fire-and-brimstone oratory, he shouted, "WELL brothers, you KNOW that WE don't sprinkle! I went out and I FOUND me a bear. And then I began to read to my bear from God's HOLY WORD! But that bear wanted nothing to do with me. So I took HOLD of him and we began to wrassle. We wrassled DOWN one hill, UP another, and DOWN another until we came to a creek. So, quick-like, I DUNKED him and BAPTIZED his hairy soul. And just like you said, he became as gentle as a lamb. We spent the rest of the day praising Jesus."

They both looked over at the rabbi, who was lying in a hospital bed. He was in a body cast and traction, with IVs and monitors running in and out of him. He was in bad shape. The rabbi looked up and said, "All things considered, circumcision may not have been the best place to begin."

———

A man and his young son went to church, and when they came out the father was complaining that the service was too long, the preacher was no good, and the singing was off-key.

Finally the little boy said, "Daddy, I thought it was pretty good for only a dime."

———

When children retell the Bible stories:

- "The people who followed the Lord were called the twelve decibels."

- "The epistles were the wives of the apostles."

- "The greatest miracle in the Bible is when Joshua told his son to stand still and he obeyed."

The pastor's good-news/bad-news day:

Good News: The women's club voted to send you a get-well card.

Bad News: The vote passed, 31-30.

Good News: The parish council accepted your job description the way you wrote it.

Bad News: They were so inspired by what it said that they're asking the bishop for a priest capable of filling the position.

Good News: The finance committee finally voted to add more church parking.

Bad News: They want to blacktop the front lawn of the rectory.

Good News: Church attendance rose dramatically over the last three weeks.

Bad News: You were on vacation.

Good News: The church youth group came to the rectory for a visit.

Bad News: It was in the middle of the night and they brought toilet paper and shaving cream.

There was an elderly deacon who had to have all of his teeth pulled and new dentures made.

The first Sunday, he only preached two minutes.

The second Sunday, he preached five minutes.

On the third Sunday, he preached for an hour and a half.

When the pastor asked him why he spoke so long, he replied, "Father, the first Sunday my gums were so sore that it hurt to talk. The second Sunday my dentures were still hurting a lot. The third Sunday, I accidentally grabbed my wife's dentures…and I couldn't shut up!"

The preacher's five-year-old daughter noticed that her deacon father always paused and bowed his head for a moment before starting his homily. One day she asked him why.

"Well, Honey," he began, proud that his daughter was so observant, "I'm asking the Lord to help me preach well."

"How come he never answers your prayer?" she asked guilelessly.

If you don't pay your exorcist, do you get repossessed?

The pastor wasn't feeling well during Mass, so he leaned over to the deacon at the last minute and asked him to preach the homily.

As he began his homily, the deacon said, "You know, a substitute preacher like me is like a piece of cardboard in a broken window. He fills the space, but he's not the real glass."

After Mass, a parishioner came up to the deacon and tried to give him a compliment. "You weren't a replacement at all, Deacon Bob," she said. "You were a real pane."

———

A priest in Florida complained that it was very difficult to get the Christian message across to his parish. "It's so beautiful here in winter," he said, "that heaven doesn't interest them. And it's so hot here in summer, that hell doesn't scare them."

———

The grade-school religious ed teacher was explaining the difference between right and wrong to her class.

"All right, children, let's take another example," she said. "If I were to get into a man's pocket and take his billfold with all his money, what would I be?"

Little Jonnie raised his hand and blurted, "His wife!"

A big, burly man knocked on the rectory door and asked to see the pastor, who was known to be a compassionate and charitable person.

"Father," he said in a broken voice, "I wish to draw your attention to the terrible plight of a poor family in the parish. Their father is dead, their mother is too ill to work, and the nine children are starving. They're about to be turned out into the cold, empty streets unless someone pays their rent."

"How terrible!" stammered the pastor. "I'll see what we can do. May I ask who you are?"

The sympathetic visitor applied his handkerchief to his eyes. "I'm the landlord," he sobbed.

———

Little Jonnie was kneeling beside his bed with his mother and grandmother and softly saying his prayers, "Dear God, please bless Mummy and Daddy and all the family and please give me a good night's sleep."

Suddenly he looked up and shouted, "AND DON'T FORGET TO GIVE ME A BICYCLE FOR MY BIRTHDAY!"

"There is no need to shout like that, little Jonnie," said his mother. "God isn't deaf."

"No," little Jonnie whispered, "but Grandma is."

"No Excuses" Sunday:

- Cots will be placed in the narthex for those who say, "Sunday is my only day to sleep in."

- There will be a special section with lounge chairs for those who feel the pews are too hard.

- Eye drops will be available for those with tired eyes from watching too much TV late Saturday night.

- We will have steel helmets for those who say, "The roof would cave in if I ever came to church."

- Blankets will be furnished for those who think the church is too cold, and fans for those who say it is too hot.

- Scorecards will be available for those who wish to keep track of all the hypocrites present. (A prominent space will be allotted at the top of the card for the cardholder to write his or her own name first.)

- We will distribute "Since When Isn't a Dollar Enough?" placards for use during the collection.

- The section by the window will be reserved for those who like to seek God in nature.

- The altar will be decorated with both Christmas poinsettias and Easter lilies for those who never have seen the church without one or the other of them.

God Is Everywhere:

He was just a little boy, on a week's first day.
He was wandering home from Mass on Sunday
    dawdling on the way.
He scuffed his shoes into the grass; he found a caterpillar.
He found a fluffy milkweed pod, and blew out all the "filler."

A bird's nest in a tree overhead, so wisely placed on high,
    was just another wonder that caught his eager eye.
A neighbor watched his zigzag course
    and hailed him from the lawn;
Asked him where he'd been that day and what was going on.

"I've been to Sunday School," he said and turned a piece of sod.
He picked up a wiggly worm replying, "I've learned a lot of God."
"A very fine way," the neighbor said, "for a boy to spend his time.
If you tell me where God is, I'll give you a brand new dime."

Quick as a flash the answer came!
Nor were his accents faint.
"I'll give you a dollar, Mister,
If you can tell me where God ain't."

———

A woman was mailing an old family Bible to her brother in another state.

"Is there anything breakable in this package?" asked the postal clerk.

"Only the Ten Commandments," the woman replied.

A Catholic woman was sitting at a stoplight this morning. The driver in front of her was yapping on his cell phone and even though the light went green he didn't move. The light turned red again. The woman wasn't happy and began cursing up a storm and pounding on her horn.

Suddenly there was a cop, gun drawn, tapping on her window. Very quickly the woman found herself in a holding cell downtown.

After about two hours, the same cop came in and told her she was free to go. "I knew it," she said smugly. "I knew you couldn't arrest me just for yelling in my own car. You haven't heard the last of this."

The cop replied, "I didn't arrest you for shouting in your car, lady. I was behind you at the light and saw you screaming and beating your steering wheel and honking your horn and then I noticed the 'What would Jesus do?' bumper sticker and decided you must have stolen the car."

Several Catholic children found a dead robin. Feeling that a proper burial should be performed, they secured a small box and some rags, dug a hole in the back yard, and made ready to dispose of the deceased.

The deacon's five-year-old son was chosen to say the prayer. And with great dignity, he intoned, "Glory be to the Father…and to the Son… and into the hole he goes."

A man bought a mule from a monk who lived at a very isolated monastery. The monk said the mule had been trained in a very special way: If you wanted to make him move, you had to shout, "Hallelujah!" And the only way to make the mule stop was to command, "Amen!"

But the price was right and the buyer was pleased with his purchase. Immediately he got on the mule to try out the monk's instructions.

"Hallelujah!" he shouted and the mule began to trot. "Amen," shouted the man and the mule stopped immediately. "This is great!" he said. With a bellowing "Hallelujah," he rode off, very happy.

As the man traveled through some mountains toward a towering cliff he suddenly forgot the word to make the mule stop.

"Exodus," the man said. Nothing.

"Jerusalem!" he cried. The mule just kept going toward the cliff.

"Oh, no. What was that word? Bible! Church! Holy Ghost!" shouted the man. The mule just began to trot faster, closer and closer to the cliff's edge.

Finally, in desperation, the man said a prayer. "Please, Lord, make this blasted mule stop before I go off the edge of this mountain. I pray this in Jesus' name, Amen."

Just then the mule abruptly stopped, just a step from the edge of the cliff.

"Hallelujah!" the man shouted.

There were two Catholic laymen shipwrecked on a desert island.

The minute they got to the island, one of them started screaming and yelling: "We're going to die! We're going to die! There's no food! No water! We're going to die!"

The second man was propped up against a palm tree and acting so calmly it drove the first man crazy.

"Don't you understand? We're going to die!" the first man said.

"You don't understand. I make $500,000 a year," said the second man.

The first man looked at him quite dumbfounded and asked: "What difference does that make? We're on an island with no food and no water! We're going to die!"

The second man answered, "You just don't get it. I make $500,000 a year and I donated one time to the diocesan stewardship fund. My bishop will find me!"

Two little boys were walking home from religious education class after hearing a story about the devil. One boy said, "What do you think about all this Satan stuff?"

The other replied, "Well, you know how Santa Claus turned out. It's probably just your dad and mom."

Deep in the uncharted South Pacific, a ship's captain spotted smoke coming from a hut on an uncharted island.

Landing on the deserted island, the rescuers were met by a single shipwreck survivor. He said, "I'm so glad you're here! I've been alone on this island for more than five years!"

The captain replied, "If you're all alone on the island, why do I see three huts?"

The survivor said, "I live in one and go to church in another."

"What about the third hut?" asked the captain.

"That's the church I used to go to before they made all the changes."

Recently at Mass, the gruff pastor's homily was just four minutes long, a fraction of his usual ramblings.

Why?

"I regret to inform the congregation," he explained from the pulpit, "that my dog, which is very fond of eating paper, ate that portion of my sermon which I was unable to deliver this morning."

Following Mass, a visitor from another parish shook hands with the pastor and said, "Father, if that dog of yours has any pups, I want to get one for my priest."

Harry Langworthy was a know-it-all and his boss was getting fed up with it, especially with his claim that he knew all sorts of famous people.

"Okay, Harry," his boss said one day. "Prove that you know famous people. Do you know Tom Cruise?"

"Oh, sure," said Harry, "me and Tom go way back."

Intrigued, Harry's boss flew both of them to Hollywood, and pretty soon they were knocking at Tom Cruise's door. The butler let them in and Tom Cruise rushed to greet them. "How's it going, Harry?" he said. "Long time, no see." They all had lunch together, discussing movies.

"Well, I'm impressed, Harry," said the boss as they left. "But I bet you don't know the President."

"Sure I do," said Harry, and with that they were off to Washington. Pretty soon, Secret Service agents escorted the pair into the Oval Office.

"Hey, Harry," said President Obama, warmly embracing his old friend.

After a nice visit and a dinner with Michelle, the boss and Harry left the White House. The boss was suitably impressed, but he was not giving up.

"Okay, Harry, if you know the pope then I'll admit you know everyone."

"Why, sure I know the pope!" said Harry. "Next stop: the Vatican."

The two of them wandered through St. Peter's Square in a crowd of thousands, and Harry said, "Heck, Benedict won't be able to see us from here. You wait here and watch up on that balcony, and I'll come out with the pope in a few minutes." So Harry went up to the Swiss Guards, whispered to them, and they opened the doors and let him into the papal palace.

About ten minutes later, the upstairs balcony opened. There was Harry standing next to a man dressed all in white. They both began to wave at the crowd.

The boss said to an old Italian woman next to him: "Scusi, but can you tell me if that man all dressed in white is really Pope Benedict XVI?"

The woman said to him in her broken English, "You meana the guy standing next to Harry Langworthy?"

———

Little Jonnie was walking down the beach when he spotted a woman sitting under an umbrella on the sand.

He walked up to her and asked, "Are you a Catholic?"

She replied, "Yes."

"Do you go to Mass regularly?" little Jonnie asked.

The woman nodded her head, "Yes, I do."

"Do you pray often?" little Jonnie asked.

Again the woman answered, "Yes."

"Okay," said little Jonnie. "Will you hold my cell phone while I go swimming?"

A recent convert to Catholicism made it a point to regularly go to confession. "I stole some lumber again, Father," he said.

"How much lumber did you steal this time?" asked the priest in an exasperated voice.

"Father, I built my dog a nice new doghouse."

The priest replied, "Well, that's not so bad...."

But the man interrupted him, adding, "Well, Father, I also built myself a four-car garage."

"Now that's a little more serious," said the priest. But the man wasn't done yet.

"Father, I've got to get it all off my chest. I built a doghouse, a four-car garage, and a five-bedroom, four-bath home!"

Shocked, the priest replied, "Well, that is most serious. I'm afraid that I'm going to have to insist that you make an entire novena as your penance."

The man looked perplexed for a bit and said, "Father, I don't know what a novena is, but if you've got the blueprints, I've got the lumber."

———

**The secret of a good homily is
to have a good beginning
and a good ending...
as close together as possible.**

A priest and a minister were driving in the minister's car to an ecumenical conference in another state when a rabbit dashed out in front of the car. The bunny was squashed flat.

The priest stopped, got out, and stood over the flattened rabbit. He took a flask of holy water from his bag, sprinkled some on the rabbit's body, and said a blessing.

The minister then got something out of his bag and poured it on the dead rabbit, which came back to life, jumped up, and hopped back into the woods, waving frantically with one paw.

The priest said, "That was a miracle! What did you pour on that poor rabbit?"

The minister looked at the bottle and read the label. It said: "Hare Restorer, with Permanent Wave."

A monastery in the English countryside had fallen on hard times, and the abbot decided to establish a business to defray their expenses. The monks first considered a bakery or a winery, but being English they decided to open a fish-and-chips restaurant. The establishment soon became very popular, attracting people from all over.

One customer, thinking himself clever, asked one of the brothers standing nearby, "I suppose you're the fish friar?"

"No," answered the brother with a straight face, "I'm the chip monk."

A pastor and one of his deacons are flying to Los Angeles for a conference. It's a long flight so the deacon leans over to his pastor and asks if he would like to play a game. The pastor just wants to take a nap, so he politely declines and turns toward the window to catch a few winks.

The deacon, a persistent fellow, explains to the priest that the game is easy and a lot of fun. "It's like this," he says. "I ask you a question, and if you don't know the answer, you pay me $5. Then you ask me a question, and if I don't know the answer, I'll pay you $5."

The priest is tired and doesn't want to play, so the deacon raises the stakes. "Okay," he says. "If you don't know the answer, you pay me $5; and if I don't know the answer, I'll pay you $50!"

Now he's got the priest's attention, who realizes the deacon isn't going to stop until he plays the game, so he agrees.

The deacon asks the first question. "What's the distance from the earth to the moon?"

The priest doesn't say a word, but reaches into his wallet, pulls out a five-dollar bill and hands it to the deacon.

Now, it's the priest's turn. He asks, "What goes up a hill with three legs and comes down on four?" Then he turns away and goes to sleep.

The deacon is baffled. He takes out his laptop computer and searches the Internet and the Library of Congress. Frustrated, he sends e-mails to his friends — all to no avail. After about an hour, he wakes the pastor and hands him $50. The priest takes the money and again closes his eyes.

The deacon won't have that. He shakes the pastor and asks, "Well, so what's the answer? What goes up a hill with three legs and comes down on four?"

"I haven't the slightest idea," the priest says, and then he reaches into his wallet, hands the deacon $5, and goes back to sleep.

———

Struggling to make ends meet, the newly ordained deacon was livid when he confronted his wife with the receipt for a $250 dress she had bought: "How could you do this?"

"I was outside the store looking at the dress in the window, and then I found myself trying it on," she explained. "It was like Satan was whispering in my ear, 'You look fabulous in that dress. Buy it!'"

"Well," the deacon replied, "You know how I deal with that kind of temptation. I say, 'Get behind me, Satan!'"

"I did," replied his wife, "but then he said, 'It looks fabulous from back here, too!'"

———

**Many folks want to serve God,
but only as advisers.**

Arthur was sitting outside his local bar one day, enjoying a quiet drink and generally feeling good about himself, when a nun suddenly appeared at his table and began proclaiming the evils of drink.

"You should be ashamed of yourself, young man! Drinking is a sin! Alcohol is the blood of the devil," she railed on and on.

After a while, Arthur began to grow annoyed. He decided to take the offensive.

"Just how do you know about the evils of drinking, Sister?" he asked.

"My mother superior told me so," she replied.

"But have you ever had a drink yourself? How can you be sure that what you're saying is true?" asked Arthur.

"Don't be ridiculous," the nun replied. "Of course I've never drunk alcohol myself."

"Then let me buy you a drink," said the young man. "Then, if you still believe it's evil, I'll give up drink for life."

The nun was aghast: "How could I sit outside this bar drinking?" she said.

"I'll get the bartender to put it in a coffee cup for you, and then no one will ever know," said the young man.

Reluctantly, the nun agreed, and Arthur went inside to the bartender and ordered another beer for himself and a triple vodka on the rocks. Then he lowered his voice and said to the bartender, "And could you put the vodka in a coffee cup?"

"Oh no," said the barkeep. "That drunken nun isn't outside again, is she?"

Father O'Malley answers the phone.

"Hello, is this Father O'Malley?" a woman's voice says.

"It is," he replies.

"This is the IRS. Can you help us?"

"I can."

"Do you know a Ted Houlihan?"

"I do."

"Is he a member of your congregation?"

"He is."

"Did he donate $10,000 to the church?"

"He will."

———

A missionary was walking in Africa when he heard the ominous padding of a lion behind him. "Oh Lord," prayed the missionary, "I surely pray that the lion walking behind me is a good Catholic lion."

Then, without looking back, the missionary heard the lion praying and felt better, until he heard: "Bless us, O Lord, and these thy gifts, which we are about to receive from thy bounty, through Christ our Lord. Amen."

A deacon who—shall we say—is "humor impaired," attended a continuing education conference designed to help encourage and better equip homilists for their ministry.

Among the speakers were many dynamic speakers. One boldly approached the pulpit and, gathering the entire crowd's attention, said, "The best years of my life were spent in the arms of a woman who wasn't my wife!"

The crowd was shocked, but the man continued, saying, "And that woman was my mother!"

The crowd burst into laughter and the preacher delivered the rest of his talk, which was a great success.

The next week, the deacon decided he'd give this humor thing a try and use that joke. He confidently approached the pulpit that sunny Sunday morning and proclaimed loudly, "The greatest years of my life were spent in the arms of a woman who was not my wife!"

The congregation was stunned into silence and the deacon got flustered. After standing silent in the pulpit for almost 10 seconds, trying to recall the second half of the joke, he finally blurted out, "And I can't remember who she was!"

———

Moses started out as a basket case.

Here's some really good advice for any new priest posted to an unfamiliar town.

Rev. Billy Graham once told of a time early in his ministry when he arrived in a small town to preach a sermon. Wanting to mail a letter, he asked a young boy where the post office was. The youth gave the directions. Graham thanked him and said, "If you'll come to the church this evening, you can hear me telling everyone how to get to heaven."

"I don't think so," the boy said. "You don't even know your way to the post office."

———

The town's big Catholic cathedral was having some extensive repair work done on its upper floors. To get material up and down, workers rigged something called a "cage elevator." A characteristic of these elevators is that the gate must be closed manually before it can be called to another floor.

On a recent afternoon one of the workers, Peter by name, took the elevator to the top floor and forgot to close the gate. Unfortunately, the elevator was needed back on the first floor. The cathedral's rector was walking by and decided to help.

That's when visitors to the cathedral were treated to the sight of the rector of the cathedral shouting up to the heavens: "Peter! PLEASE CLOSE THE GATE!"

The little boy spotted a priest and asked him, "Why do you dress so funny?"

"This is the uniform I wear when I work," the priest said patiently.

The boy considered that and asked, "Do you have a boo-boo?"

The priest was puzzled, but quickly figured out that the boy was looking at his Roman collar. The priest pulled out the white plastic insert and showed it to the child, telling him that it was also part of his uniform.

On the back side of the collar there was some writing: "Wash with warm soapy water."

The priest showed this to the little boy and then asked him, "Do you know what these words say?"

The little boy, obviously too young to read, said, "I sure do." The priest was surprised but said, "Okay then, tell me what they say."

"Kills fleas and ticks for up to six months," the boy replied.

A bishop was visiting another diocese to give a series of talks to various groups. There was a welcoming dinner for him, which was covered by a reporter for the local Catholic newspaper. The bishop gave a brief talk sharing several anecdotes.

Because he expected to use the jokes again, he asked the reporter not to include them in his story.

So the reporter ended his article thus: "The bishop also told several stories that cannot be published."

There is a story about a monastery in Europe perched high on a cliff hundreds of feet in the air. The only way to reach the monastery was to be suspended in a basket that was pulled to the top by several monks who tugged with all their strength.

Obviously the ride up the steep cliff in that basket was terrifying. About halfway up, one tourist became nervous when he noticed that the rope was old and frayed.

With a trembling voice he asked the monk with him in the basket how often they changed the rope. The monk thought for a moment and answered, "Whenever it breaks."

An old $1 bill and an even older $20 bill arrive at a Federal Reserve Bank to be retired.

"I've had a pretty good life," the $20 says. "I've been to Vegas, the finest restaurants in New York, and even went on a Caribbean cruise."

"You certainly did have an exciting life!" the $1 says.

"Yes, I have," responds the $20. "What have you done in your life?"

"Oh, I spent my entire life at a Catholic church. I'm the $1 the pastor complained was being donated every week."

"Wait," the $20 interrupts. "What's a Catholic church?"

The new pastor stood at the church door greeting parishioners as they left following his first Mass after being appointed by the bishop. The comments were generally welcoming, except for one man who said, "That was a very dull and boring homily, Father."

A few minutes later, the same man showed up in the line again and said, "Father, I don't think you gave much thought to what you had to say this morning."

Minutes later, the same man appeared again in the line, this time muttering, "You really blew it, Father."

Finally, the priest could stand it no longer. He called the deacon over and asked who the man was.

"Him? Oh, that's Oliver. Don't let him bother you," said the deacon. "He's a little slow. All he does is repeat whatever he hears other people saying."

———

At the pearly gates, St. Peter greeted a priest and a congressman and gave them their room assignments.

"Father, here are the keys to one of our nicest efficiency units," Peter said with a smile. "And for you, Mr. Congressman, here are the keys to our finest penthouse suite."

The priest didn't want to appear disappointed, but the look on his face gave it away. St. Peter took him aside and said, "Listen, Father, priests are a dime a dozen up here, but this is the first congressman we've ever seen."

Three permanent deacons — who in their regular careers were a mechanic, a pharmacist, and a salesman — agreed that people were always coming up to them with their problems, but that they had no one to turn to with theirs.

So they decided to share their deepest, darkest sins with one another.

The mechanic admitted that he was a compulsive shopper, deeply in debt. "That's why I always overcharge my customers at the garage," he said.

The pharmacist said he had a drug problem. "As a result," he said, "I fake prescriptions to get drugs for myself."

The salesman said: "I know it's wrong, but no matter how hard I try, I just can't keep a secret."

When the diocesan information technology people checked the parish computers for security problems, they found that the youth minister was using the following password for her computer: MickeyMinniePlutoHueyLouieDeweyDonaldGoofy.

When the technician asked why she had such a long password, she said, "Helllloooooooooo! You guys in support said that it had to be at least eight characters long, didn't you?"

The Catholic school teacher looked out at her room full of students and saw that little Jonnie appeared ready to burst into tears. Compassion goes with the territory, so the young teacher asked little Jonnie what was wrong.

"It's my grandfather," Jonnie blurted out as he dissolved into sobs. "He's gone away forever."

Ever ready to console, the teacher gently said to the student, "All of us are so sorry to hear that, Jonnie. But I'm sure your grandfather is in a better place now."

Deciding to bring a little religious education into the conversation, the teacher asked the rest of the class, "Does anyone know where Jonnie's grandfather is now?"

"Yes, I do," replied one of the other students. "He's in prison!"

Possible signs outside of church:

- Gambling is a sin. Bet you can't give it up.

- There are some questions that can't be answered by Google.

- Let us help you study for your final exam.

- Speak well of your enemies. After all, you created them.

- The meek shall inherit the earth, that is, if you don't mind.

- Happy Easter to our Christian friends. Happy Passover to our Jewish friends. Happy Ramadan to our Muslim friends. To our atheist friends, good luck.

A bishop was having a reception at the diocese's ministry center, called the John Paul Auditorium, a fine old building with high ceilings. A string quartet was playing in a corner, but because the acoustics were so fine, the music flowed throughout.

A visitor attended the reception and was quite impressed with both the architecture and the acoustics. He asked the diocesan director of development, "Of course, this magnificent auditorium is named for the late pope, right?"

"No," replied the director, "it's named after John Paul, the business writer."

"Never heard of him," snorted the visitor. "What did he write?"

"A check," said the development director.

Two hippies were walking down the street and passed a priest with his arm in a sling.

"Hey, man," said one of the hippies, "what happened to you?"

"I slipped in the bathtub and broke my arm," replied the priest.

"Ouch, man, that must have hurt," said the other hippie. "Hope you're feeling better."

"Thank you for your good wishes," said the priest. "God bless you."

When the hippies got out of earshot, one said to the other, "Man, what's a bathtub?"

"I don't know," said the other. "I'm not Catholic."

In the Garden of Eden, in that brief, happy period before the Fall, the First Man and the God who created him would sometimes talk things over in the shade of a big tree.

"Why did you make Woman so beautiful?" Adam asked.

"So you would love her," God answered.

Adam thought about that a while.

"Then why did you have to make her so dumb?" Adam wondered.

"So she would love you," came the reply.

A confirmed-atheist college professor announced that he was going to prove to the students that there was no God.

Standing at his lectern he announced loudly, "God, if you're real, I want you to knock me off this platform. I'll give you 15 minutes!"

As the clock ticked away the minutes, the professor kept taunting God, saying, "Here I am God; I'm still waiting."

When there was only about a minute left, a hulking 250-pound linebacker for the university's football team came running from his seat in the back of the room, tackled the professor, and sent him flying off the platform.

"God was busy," said the football player.

A pastor, the associate pastor, the parish deacon, and a layman were playing golf one morning. Unfortunately, it was a slow round as they found themselves constantly waiting for a particularly slow group of golfers in front of them.

The associate pastor, who was known for his impatience, fumed, "What's with those jerks? We're waiting 15 minutes between shots!"

The pastor spotted the golf course's greens keeper and asked him, "What's wrong with that group ahead of us? They're rather slow, aren't they?"

"Yes," conceded the greens keeper. "But that's a group of blind firefighters. They lost their sight saving our clubhouse from a fire last year, so we let them play for free whenever they want."

Embarrassed, the group fell silent, except for the associate pastor.

"So why can't they play at night?" he asked.

One Sunday morning as he arrived for Mass, the deacon was met in the sacristy by the pastor. "Deacon," he said sternly, "I've been told that you went to the ball game last Sunday instead of coming to Mass."

"That's a lie," said the deacon, "and I have the fish at home to prove it!"

A group of poor friars lived on a secluded mountain. Because they had little money, they needed to come up with a way to earn some. One day they cut some lovely flowers from their gardens, took the blooms to the local marketplace, and sold them. They made $25.

The venture was so successful that soon the friars brought flowers to the market every day. In no time, they had earned more than $1,000. But when their provincial learned of the business he was furious. He lectured the friars about the evils of money and forbade them from selling more flowers.

But instead of obeying, the friars rebelled and continued to peddle their flowers in town.

Finally, the provincial was forced to hire a guard named Hugh to make the naughty friars stop their sales. It took two years, but when the provincial was finally convinced the flower sales had ended, he let the guard go.

However, as soon the friars discovered that Hugh wasn't watching any longer, they went right back into the flower business. It was more lucrative than ever.

When word of this came to the provincial, he was furious. His assistant suggested that they hire Hugh again.

"You're right," the provincial agreed solemnly. "Only Hugh can prevent florist friars."

**It is easier to preach ten lousy sermons
than to live one good one.**

Father O'Malley, recently transferred to a mission parish in Texas, rose from his bed one morning. It was a fine spring day. He walked to the window to get a deep breath of the beautiful day outside.

That's when he noticed the jackass lying dead in the middle of the rectory's front lawn.

He immediately phoned the local police station. The conversation went like this.

"Good morning. This is Sergeant Jones. How might I help you?"

"And the best of the day t'yerself, Sergeant. This is Father O'Malley at St. Ann's. There's a jackass lying dead in me front lawn."

Sergeant Jones, who was a Protestant and considered himself to be quite a wit, replied with a smirk, "Well now, Father, it was always my impression that you Cat'lic priests took care of the last rites for one of your own!"

There was silence on the line for a long moment before Father O'Malley replied: "Aye, Sergeant, 'tis certainly true that we take care of our own; but we are also obliged to notify the next of kin."

Going over the parish's records, the bookkeeper found a suspicious receipt from a local paint store signed by someone named Fred Christian. He wasn't aware of anyone by that name who would be buying paint for the parish, so he called the store.

"I'm sorry," he told the manager, "but I don't believe there are any Christians here at St. John's Parish."

The pastor's sermon lasted its usual half-hour. After Mass, a man came up and shook his hand.

"Father, that was an inspirational message," he said.

"Thank you," replied the priest.

"It was so poetic and so meaningful," the man went on.

"How kind of you," said the pastor, quite embarrassed.

"But such a shame," said the man, frowning.

"A shame?" said the priest, now pretty confused. "Why?"

"Well, I'm a TV producer, and we run a daily 'Two Minute Devotional' on the local Catholic network. Your sermon would be perfect, but I don't see how it would fit."

"No problem," said the priest. "I can say the same thing in two minutes."

"So why don't you?" asked the man.

———

Three Kinds of Catholics:

- Conservative Catholics believe nothing should be done that hasn't already been done.
- Moderate Catholics believe something should be done, but not quite yet.
- Liberal Catholics believe everything should have been done yesterday.

Bubba was a confirmed atheist who loved the racetrack. One day he was losing all his bets when he noticed a priest step out onto the track and bless the forehead of one of the horses lining up for the fourth race. Lo and behold, the horse — a very long shot — won.

The next race, Bubba watched as the priest stepped out onto the track before the fifth race lined up and blessed one of the horses.

Bubba made a beeline for the window and placed a small bet on the horse. Sure enough, the horse, another long shot, won.

Bubba collected his winnings and waited to see which horse the priest blessed in the next race. The priest showed, blessed a horse, Bubba bet on it, and it won!

All day, every horse the priest blessed won and so did Bubba.

By the last race, he knew his dreams were going to come true. He made a quick stop at the ATM and withdrew his entire savings. In the final race, the priest again stepped onto the track and blessed the forehead, eyes, ears, and hooves of one of the horses.

Bubba bet every cent.

The horse came in dead last.

Bubba was dumbfounded. He found the priest and demanded, "What happened? All day you blessed horses and they won. The last race, you blessed a horse and he lost. Now I've lost my life's savings."

"That's the problem with you atheists," said the priest. "You can't tell the difference between a blessing and the Last Rites."

A drunk stumbles into the local parish during the Easter Vigil while the pastor is baptizing new Catholics, briefly immersing their heads under water in the baptismal font. The drunk nearly trips on the font and bumps into the pastor, who thinks he's one of the catechumens. Though the priest is almost overcome by the smell of booze, he asks the drunk, "Are you ready to find Jesus?"

"Yes, I am," replies the drunk. So the pastor dunks him. He pulls him up and asks, "Have you found Jesus?"

"No," says the drunk, "I haven't." So the pastor dunks him again, longer this time. He pulls him out of the water and asks again, "Have you found Jesus?"

The drunk again answers, "No."

By now the priest is getting a little frustrated, so he immerses the drunk again, but this time he holds him down for about 30 seconds.

When the drunk begins kicking his legs and thrashing his arms, the pastor brings him back up out of the water and cries, "For the love of God, man, have you found Jesus?"

The drunk wipes his eyes and catches his breath and asks, "Father, are you sure this is where he fell in?"

**Quit griping about the Church;
if it were perfect, you couldn't be a member.**

Four Catholic women are having coffee. The first tells her friends, "My son is a priest. When he walks into a room, everyone calls him 'Father.'"

The second woman chirps, "My son is a bishop. Whenever he walks into a room, people say, 'Your Excellency.'"

The third says smugly, "My son is a cardinal. Whenever he walks into a room, people say, 'Your Eminence.'"

The fourth woman sips her coffee in silence. She finally says, "My son is a gorgeous, 6-foot-2-inch male model. When he walks into a room, people say, 'Oh my God....'"

Three very competitive priests died, but before God would let them into heaven, he gave them a chance to be anything they wanted.

The first priest said, "I want to come back as myself, but 100 times smarter than I already am."

So God made him 100 times smarter.

The second priest said, "I want to be even better than that priest — make me 1,000 times smarter than I already am."

So God made him 1,000 times smarter.

The last guy decided he would be the best. So he said, "God, make me better than both of them. Make me a million times smarter than I already am."

So God made him a woman.

**Most people assume WWJD is for "What Would Jesus Do?"
But the initials really stand for "What Would Jesus Drive?"**

- One theory is that Jesus would tool around in an old Plymouth because "the Bible says God drove Adam and Eve out of the Garden of Eden in a Fury."

- But in Psalm 83, the Almighty clearly owns a Pontiac and a Geo. The passage urges the Lord to "pursue your enemies with your Tempest and terrify them with your Storm."

- Perhaps God favors Dodge pickup trucks, because Moses' followers are warned not to go up a mountain "until the Ram's horn sounds a long blast."

- Some scholars insist that Jesus drove a Honda but didn't like to talk about it. As proof, they cite a verse in the Gospel of John where Christ tells the crowd, "For I did not speak of my own Accord."

- Meanwhile, Moses rode an old British motorcycle, as evidenced by a Bible passage declaring, "the roar of Moses' Triumph is heard in the hills."

- Likewise, Joshua drove a Triumph sports car, but this one obviously had a hole in its muffler, because "Joshua's Triumph was heard throughout the land."

**Some Catholics' minds are like concrete:
thoroughly mixed up and permanently set.**

The parish's liturgy director had a reputation for a hot temper. Somehow the local weekly newspaper got wrong information and printed her obituary.

She stormed into the newspaper office and demanded, "The report of my death in your paper is a lie. I'll sue you for everything you've got if you don't apologize in your next issue."

The next edition contained the following notice: "We regret very much that the notice of Mary Smith's death, which appeared in our last issue, was not true."

Three lay women died and were taken by God to the top of a cliff. God told them that because they had lived exemplary lives they would be given one chance to become anything they desired.

The first woman shouted, "I want to be an eagle." She ran to the edge of the cliff, jumped into the air, and instantly became an eagle and soared off into the sunset.

The second woman shouted, "I want to be an owl." She ran to the edge of the cliff, jumped into the air, and instantly became an owl and soared off into the sunset.

The third woman shouted, "I want to be an angel." She ran towards the edge of the cliff, tripped on a rock and instantly became a fallen angel.

A pastor explained to his congregation that the parish budget was in the red, so he asked them to consider being more generous. He offered that whoever gave the most money that day would be able to pick three songs for Mass the following Sunday.

When the offering was brought up to the altar, the pastor glanced down and noticed that someone had dropped in $500. He was so excited that he immediately said he'd like to personally thank the person who made the donation.

A very quiet, saintly old lady in the back of the church shyly raised her hand. The pastor asked her to come up to the altar. She slowly she made her way towards him. The pastor told her how wonderful it was that she gave so much and asked her to pick out three hymns for next Sunday.

The old woman's eyes brightened as she looked over the congregation. She pointed to the three most handsome men in the church and said, "I'll take him, him, and him."

———

A mother was teaching her four-year-old daughter the Lord's Prayer. For several evenings at bedtime the little girl repeated it after her mother. One night the girl said she was finally ready to do it solo. The mother listened with pride as she carefully enunciated each word right up to the end. "Lead us not into temptation," the little girl prayed, "and deliver us some email, Amen."

A priest was walking down the street when he spotted about a dozen boys, all between 10 and 12 years of age who were gathered around a little dog.

Concerned that the kids might be harming the animal, the priest went over and asked, "What are you boys doing with that dog?"

One replied, "This dog is just an old neighborhood stray, Father. We all want to take him home, but only one of us can have him. So we've decided that whichever one of us can tell the biggest fib will get to keep it."

The priest was shocked. "You shouldn't be having a contest telling fibs," he said, and then he launched into a ten-minute homily against lying. He ending it, saying, "Why, when I was your age, I never told a lie."

There was dead silence for about a minute. Just as the priest was beginning to think he'd gotten through to them, the smallest boy gave a deep sigh and said, "All right, give him the dog."

———

The sixth-grade religious education teacher was telling the Bible story of Sodom and Gomorrah, explaining that when Lot's wife looked back she turned into a pillar of salt.

Suddenly little Jonnie interrupted, saying, "My mommy looked back once while she was driving," he announced, "and she turned into a telephone pole."

A pious Catholic woman was at work when her babysitter called to say that her daughter was ill. The frantic woman left work immediately and stopped by the pharmacy for medication, but when she returned to her car she discovered she had locked the keys inside.

She didn't know what to do, so she called the babysitter who suggested, "You might find a coat hanger to open the door."

The woman found a rusty coat hanger on the side of the road, looked at it, and realized, "I don't know how to use this."

All she had left was prayer. She bowed her head and asked God to send her some help. Five minutes later an old car pulled up. The dirty, bearded driver was wearing an old biker skull rag on his head. The woman glanced up to heaven and silently asked, "This is what you sent to help me?"

The man asked if he could help. She said, "Yes, my daughter is very sick. I locked my keys in my car. Please, can you use this hanger to unlock my car?"

He said, "Sure." He walked over to the car, and in less than three seconds the car was opened. She hugged the man and through her tears she said, "Thank you so much! You are a very nice man."

He replied, "Lady, I'm not a nice man. I just got out of prison today. I was convicted of car theft and have only been out for about an hour."

Sobbing, she hugged the man again and cried out loud, "Thank you, God! You even sent me a professional!"

One day Jesus' secretary came into his office in heaven and said, "Sir, you should take some time off from all of your work. Get out and meet your people. Have a good time."

That seemed like a good idea, so Jesus walked down the golden streets, shaking hands and signing autographs. Along a side street, he heard the sounds of hammering and sawing and spotted sawdust drifting from a little shop. Inside, he found a bearded carpenter working so hard the drops of perspiration were running down his face and mixing with the sawdust.

Jesus said to the man, "Why are you working so hard? Rest and enjoy yourself."

The old man said, "Oh, no, please let me continue. You see, I had a son on earth whose birth was a miracle. But I haven't been able to find him here yet. My son knew I was a carpenter, and I thought if he heard me working here he would find me."

Jesus stared at the man, and his eyes started to mist. The man stared back.

"Father?" Jesus asked.

"Pinocchio?" the man replied.

A catechist told her class, "We have been learning about how powerful the kings and queens were in biblical times. But there is a higher power. Who can tell me what it is?"

Little Jonnie blurted out, "I know! I know! Aces!"

Bill Gates died in a car accident and found himself in purgatory being sized up by God.

"Well, Bill, I'm really confused. I'm not sure whether to send you to heaven or hell. After all, you enormously helped society by putting a computer in almost every home and you were very generous with your money. Yet you created that ghastly Vista operating system, but you repented and gave us Windows 7. So I'm going to do something I've never done before. I'm going to let you decide where you want to go!"

Bill replied, "Well, thanks, God, but what's the difference between the two?"

God offered to let him view both places so he could choose.

Bill said, "Okay, then, let's try hell first."

So God brought hell up on his computer, and Bill saw a beautiful, clean, sandy beach with clear waters. There were thousands of beautiful women running around, playing in the water, laughing and frolicking about. The sun was shining, the temperature was perfect. Bill was very pleased.

"This is great!" he told God. "If this is hell, then I really want to see heaven!"

"Fine," said God and he brought heaven up on the screen. Heaven was a high place in the clouds with angels drifting about playing harps and singing. It was nice, but not nearly as enticing as hell.

"I think I prefer hell," he told God.

"Fine," said God. "As you desire."

So Bill Gates went to hell. Two weeks later, God decided to check up on the late billionaire to see how he was doing. When God arrived in hell, he found Bill shackled to a wall, screaming in the hot flames in a dark cave.

"So, Bill," God said. "How are things going?"

"This is awful," Bill said. "What happened to that other place with the beaches and the beautiful women playing in the water?"

God said, "Oh, sorry. That was just the screen saver."

In a small southern town there was a nativity scene that was very beautiful. Except for one thing. The three wise men were wearing firemen's helmets.

No one had a good explanation until a reporter from the North asked the local woman who had created it why the wise men were dressed like firemen. She began yelling, "You durn Yankees never do read the Bible!" She brought out her copy, opened it, and pointed at a passage. "See, it says right here, 'The three wise men came from afar.'"

Did you hear about the dyslexic devil worshippers?

They sold their souls to Santa.

During sharing at a parish retreat a very wealthy man stood up and told about his faith. "I'm a millionaire," he said, "and I attribute it all to the rich blessings of God in my life. I remember the turning point in my faith. I had just earned my first dollar. When I went to Mass that Sunday, the homilist was a missionary priest who told about his work. I knew that I only had a dollar bill and had to either give it all to God's work or nothing at all. So at that moment I decided to give everything I had to God. I believe that God blessed that decision, and that is why I am a rich man today."

The man finished his testimony and there was an awed silence at his words. As he returned to his seat, a little old lady in the same pew leaned over and said to him, "I dare you to do it again."

The elderly priest was surprised when he arrived in heaven and discovered that a New York cab driver had been awarded a higher place than he.

"I don't understand," he complained to God. "I devoted my entire life to the Church."

"Our policy here is to reward results," God explained. "Now, did your parishioners listen attentively when you preached a homily?"

"Well," the priest had to admit, "some people did fall asleep from time to time."

"Exactly," said God. "And when people rode in this man's taxi, they not only stayed awake, they prayed as if their lives depended on it."

A Catholic lay woman whose life hadn't exactly been a model of sainthood died and was greeted at heaven's gate by St. Peter. Her destination was hell, St. Peter told her in no uncertain terms, but at least she would be able to choose among the three hells he would show her.

The first hell was very hot and she saw people burning in fire and screaming. The next was freezing cold and she saw people shivering and crying out for relief. In the third hell, she saw people who looked quite happy despite standing in excrement up to their waists. They were drinking coffee and chatting.

That's not too bad, she thought, despite the smell. So she said to St. Peter, "I choose the third hell."

And POOF, that's where she went. She grabbed a cup of coffee and felt comfortable — until there was an announcement over a loudspeaker: "Attention. Attention. Coffee break is over. It's time to stand on your heads again."

It was Palm Sunday but because of a sore throat, little Jonnie stayed home with a sitter. When the family returned home, they were carrying several palm fronds. Little Jonnie asked them what they were for.

"People held them over Jesus' head as he walked by," his father told him.

"Wouldn't you know it?" little Jonnie fumed. "The one Sunday I don't go and he shows up."

Lying in a hospital bed, a dying man began to flail about trying to speak. The priest, keeping watch at the side of his bed, leaned quietly over and asked, "Do you have something you would like to say?"

The man nodded, so the priest handed him a pad and pen. "I know you can't speak," the priest said, "but use this to write a note and I'll give it to your wife. She's waiting just outside."

With his last bit of strength, the man took the pad and pencil and scrawled a message that he stuffed into the priest's hands. Then, with a final gasp, he died.

After administering the last rites, the priest left to break the sad news to the wife.

Consoling her, the priest handed her the note.

"Here were his last words. Just before passing on, he wrote this message to you."

The wife tearfully opened the note, which read: "TELL THIS IDIOT HE'S STANDING ON MY OXYGEN HOSE!"

Following Mass one Sunday, a young couple talked to the deacon about joining the parish. The deacon hadn't met the husband before, and asked where he'd been worshipping God before this.

After a short hesitation, the young man stammered and mumbled, "The Municipal Golf Course?"

Attending a wedding Mass for the first time, a little girl whispered to her mother, "Why is the bride dressed in white?"

"Because white is the color of happiness, and today is the happiest day of her life."

The child thought about this for a moment, then said, "So why is the groom wearing black?"

One night his mother told little Jonnie to go out to the back porch and bring in the broom.

He said, "Mama, I'm afraid to go out there. It's dark."

His mother smiled reassuringly. "You don't have to be afraid of the dark, Jonnie," she said. "Jesus is always there. He'll protect you."

Little Jonnie looked at his mother and asked, "Are you sure Jesus is out there?"

"Yes, I'm sure," she said. "He's everywhere, and he's always ready to help you when you need him."

Little Jonnie thought about that for a minute, went to the back door, and cracked it open just a little. Peering out into the darkness, he called, "Jesus? Would you please hand me the broom?"

Sign at the entrance of one Catholic church: "We provide hearing aids for those who can't hear the homilist, and cotton for those who can!"

On their way to celebrate their nuptial Mass, a young couple was involved in a car accident and died. In a flash, they found themselves sitting outside the Pearly Gates waiting for St. Peter to process them into heaven.

As they waited, they wondered if, since they never made it to the church on earth, they might be able to get married in heaven. So when St. Peter showed up, that was the first thing they asked him.

St. Peter answered, "Gee, I don't know. This is the first time anyone has asked. Let me go find out."

The couple waited and waited and waited. Two months passed, and they were still waiting. And the more they waited the more they began to doubt, wondering about the truly eternal aspect of being married in heaven. "Till death do us part" is one thing, but "forever and ever and ever" is another thing, they both thought.

"What if it doesn't work out?" they wondered. "Would we really be bound together for eternity?"

Finally, after another month of waiting, St. Peter finally returned looking bedraggled. "Yes," he informed the couple, "you can get married in heaven. Congratulations!"

"Great!" they said, "But we've been thinking, what if things don't work out for all eternity? Could we also get a divorce in heaven?"

At that, St. Peter became so angry that he slammed his clipboard into a nearby cloud. "What's wrong?" asked the frightened couple.

"OH, COME ON!" shouted St. Peter. "It took me three months to find a priest up here! Do you have any idea how long it'll take me to find a canon lawyer?"

A Catholic priest in civilian clothes waited in line to have his car filled with gas just before a long holiday weekend. He was finally able to pull up to an open pump.

A harried man getting gas at the next pump said to the priest, "Wow, it seems as if everyone waits until the last minute to get ready for a long trip."

The priest just chuckled. "I know what you mean," he said. "It's the same in my business."

While driving through rural Pennsylvania, a Catholic family caught up to an Amish carriage. The owner of the carriage obviously had a sense of humor, because attached to the back of the carriage was a hand-printed sign: "Energy-efficient vehicle: Runs on oats and grass. Caution: Do not step in exhaust."

The Catholic family also had a sense of humor and passed the carriage in their SUV. The bumper sticker on the back of their car read: "Remember man, it is our dust thou art eating."

An elderly Catholic woman had never married. After she died, her will stipulated that there be no male pallbearers at her funeral Mass. She wrote, "They wouldn't take me out while I was alive. I don't want them to take me out when I'm dead."

ABOUT THE AUTHORS

Deacon Tom Sheridan

As a veteran secular newspaperman, Tom Sheridan developed a keen eye for the humor in life. A deacon ordained in 1979 for the Diocese of Joliet, Illinois, and a former editor of the Archdiocese of Chicago's newspaper and other publications, Deacon Tom also knows a little about the humor to be found in religion. And as a husband and father of five children and several grandchildren, he believes humor will help see us all through our various struggles. He writes from Ocala, Florida, where he lives with his wife, Kathy. He is the author of *The Book of Catholic Jokes*, *The Gift of Baptism*, and *The Gift of Godparents* for ACTA Publications.

Father Paul Boudreau

Before becoming a priest, Paul Boudreau was a professional motorcycle racer, a job he says gave him a good feel for working on Sundays. Ordained in 1983 for the Diocese of Norwich, Connecticut, Father Paul has served as pastor, teacher, speaker, and journalist. His books include *Between Sundays: Daily Gospel Reflections and Prayers*, (Twenty-Third Publications); *The Path to Forgiveness* (Bayard Publications); and *The Forgiveness Book: A Catholic Approach*, co-authored with Alice Camille, (ACTA Publications). He now works for the Diocese of Stockton, California, as administrator of St. Joseph Church in the mountain community of Mammoth Lakes.

Also Available from ACTA Publications

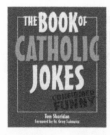
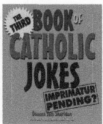
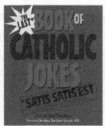